REVOLT

The Secret History of a
Natural Impulse

Loretta Graziano Breuning, PhD
Inner Mammal Institute

Dedicated to

people who forage for facts

instead of

running with the herd

Contents

1

The Joy of Revolt

People seek power because the brain rewards you with happy chemicals when you get it. Everyone has this impulse, not just politicians. The urge for social power is easy to see in others, but it's useful to see it in yourself and your loved ones. Political trends come from the urges of regular people.

Revolts are rooted in the biological urge for social dominance. Here is a brief introduction to the mammal brain's impulses beneath the verbal brain's political expression. (The biology is fully explained in my other books and at InnerMammalInstitute.org).

Human emotions are controlled by brain structures inherited from earlier mammals. This "limbic system" rewards you with a good feeling when you do something good for your survival, and alarms you with a threatened feeling when you see a survival threat. Social dominance promotes survival in the state of nature, so the limbic brain rewards you with a good feeling when you put yourself in the one-up position. We repeat behaviors that feel good, but we don't know why because the limbic system doesn't report its responses in words.

When you see yourself in the one-down position, a threat chemical is released. It feels like the external world is putting you down even though you have created the feeling internally. We don't intend to think this way, but we've inherited the operating system of earlier mammals. Humans have struggled throughout history to manage a brain that cares urgently about social dominance.

> **It feels like the external world is putting you down even though you have created the feeling internally.**

Each brain defines social dominance with neural pathways built from its own lived experience. In the modern world, we're less likely to define it with hand-to-hand brawls, and more likely to define it with pride in our skills and moral superiority. But as social creatures, we are influenced by the way those around us define it.

Animals cooperate as well as compete. They cooperate when it promotes their survival. Animals rarely fight because the risk of getting hurt triggers threat chemicals. They only fight when they think they can win. They are very good at judging their relative strength thanks to childhood tussles we call "play." When an animal sees that it's weaker than another, it restrains itself with threat chemicals. When it sees that it's stronger, happy chemicals are released and it asserts itself. Conflict only erupts when both critters perceive themselves as stronger.

Natural selection built a brain that constantly compares itself to others and responds with life-or-death feelings. You don't think this in words because the mammal brain cannot process language. Your inner mammal is literally not on speaking terms with your verbal brain. This leaves your conscious brain struggling to explain your own responses. You mirror the explanations of others because we're born with mirror neurons.

When I went to college, I learned to explain emotions the "progressive" way. I was taught that social injustice is the root cause of bad feelings, and that "social change" is the path to good feelings. My professors said we must "change the system" before we can be happy, and they meant "the capitalist system." I heard the same message in every course, so I learned it well. As a teenager, I was receptive to the idea that it's ethical to ignore your parents because they are part of a bad system.

Today, when I hear strong emotions, I hear the words I learned in college. I know the words come from Karl Marx because he was quoted so much in my

Ivy-League education. Marx's view was cited on every topic, as if we were in bible school and Marx was the bible.

Marx said that good things will come if we rise up and tear down the system. He encouraged his followers to mob the streets and riot in order to bring change. Many of his followers were shot or imprisoned, but the worldwide movement kept growing. Why?

Marxism appeals to our natural mammalian impulses. It tells you to blame "the rich" for all your frustrations, and dispossess them to get the good life. He called it "revolution," but his heirs have repackaged it with the more marketable word "justice."

Marxists had their first big win with the Russian Revolution of 1917. Worldwide socialists ecstatically anticipated the fall of all capitalist governments. They had been organizing for half a century by then, so they ardently longed for the promised land that would put them in power. They saw Russia (renamed the Soviet Union) as a beacon of hope, and proof that Marx's theories were correct.

But the 1920s disappointed socialists. Workers failed to mob the streets the way Marx had predicted. What was wrong? Marx expected socialism to attract armies of oppressed workers, but it attracted rich kids and their pub friends. This may seem surprising until you learn that Karl Marx was a rich kid himself.

Workers were busy feeding their kids, but Marx actually abandoned his kids to incite revolution. He built his theories on the work of Jean-Jacques Rousseau, who had also abandoned his kids. These philosophers condemned the ethics of "the rich," but regarded themselves as above the rules because they were saving the world. Their movement attracted people with similar ethics.

Marx had an interesting problem. Social mobility was rare before he was born, but Marx's father belonged to a new generation that could earn wealth and power without being born into the aristocracy. Young Karl would have to earn his own way instead of getting an inheritance. The risk of downward mobility is the flip side of upward mobility. But Marx created an alternative: he put himself in the one-up position by condemning "the rich". Recruiting followers to overthrow capitalism creates the good feeling of social importance without the tedium of a day job. It doesn't pay the bills, of course, so Marx spent his life begging rich people for loans.

It's easy to see how Marx's message would attract other rich kids. Of course, invoking the "greater good" to justify self-interested behavior has always been with us. Marx just shaped it in a way that appeals to the Enlightenment verbal brain while also appealing to the mammal brain. Marxism satisfies the urge for a herd by focusing on solidarity among the oppressed. It satisfies the foraging impulse with vivid images of greener pasture after "the revolution." And it satisfies the urge for social dominance without the strictures of old institutions. (These urges are detailed in all my other books.)

When capitalism did not fall as predicted, the movement changed its strategy. Socialist leaders decided that "the masses" needed training to see how oppressed they are. The timing was good. The Great Depression of the 1930s made it easier to sell the victim mindset. New media (first radio and then movies) allowed mass messaging on an unprecedented scale. By the end of the 1930s, the progressive movement was massive worldwide.

The strategy worked by targeting three institutions: education, journalism, and culture (meaning the arts and entertainment). Socialists penetrated the top echelons of these institutions and redirected them. They redirected education to teach that fighting "the rich" is the proper focus of life. They redirected journalism and the arts to glorify

Socialists penetrated the top echelons of culture and redirected it to teach that fighting "the rich" is the proper focus of life.

progressives and vilify people who earn money by selling things.

They also relabeled the mission with comforting language. Instead of focusing on violent revolution, they created a wide array of groups for different tastes. They lured "do-gooders" with lofty language, and then channeled more committed individuals into "revolutionary action." Today, the comforting language is so ingrained in our information environment that you don't think of it as Marxism. You just think of it as intelligence and virtue. You equate progressivism with peace and love, and blame any aggression on "right-wingers."

You may find it hard to believe that cultural elites are just following a script written long ago. Your teachers never said they were Marxist, and your media don't either. They suggest they are saving us from the threat posed by capitalists. They must stick to this message to keep their jobs. Teachers learn to do this in their credentialing programs, and media professionals learn in their competitive job market. Anyone who deviates from the script is ridiculed and shunned, and if they keep it up, attacked. Few people want to risk that.

It's hard to imagine yourself following a script written long ago. But when you know the template, you can see how your information is forced into it.

Here is a short, simple introduction to the progressive template.

In the mid-1700s, Jean-Jaques Rousseau said that "Man is born free but is everywhere in chains." He said that humans are effortlessly happy in the state of nature, and society is the cause of all unhappiness. His work was very popular and quickly spread by a new form of social media called "newspapers." Soon, critiquing society marked you as an intellectual.

A century later, Karl Marx said: "Rise, slaves, you have nothing to lose but your chains." His work was very popular and quickly spread by a new form of social media– posters and cheap pamphlets. Soon, condemning "the rich" gave you prestige with the intellectual in-crowd.

A century later, Saul Alinsky wrote: "It's up to us to go in and rub raw the sores of discontent, galvanize them for radical social change…The organizer's first job is to create the issues or problems, and organizations must be based on many issues. The organizer must first rub raw the resentments of the people of the community; fan the latent hostilities of many of the people to the point of overt expression. He must search out controversy and issues, rather than avoid them, for unless there is controversy people are not concerned enough to act. . . . An organizer must stir up dissatisfaction and discontent."

" An organizer must stir up dissatisfaction and discontent. "
- Saul Alinsky

Alinsky's work was very popular, especially with college professors. His message soon became a staple of the curriculum. You had to embrace Alinsky's views in order to be considered an educated person. Hillary Clinton wrote her senior thesis on Alinsky, and Barack Obama joined the community organizing program Alinsky created after college.

Alinsky updated the progressive message by stripping charged words like "socialism," "communism," and "Marxism." He focused on "the enemy" without naming the enemy. Thus, his handbook is useful for inciting revolution anywhere, which was his intent.

Nixon was president when I was in college and I soon learned to see him as the enemy. When Reagan was president, I learned to see him as the enemy too. By the time George W. Bush came along, I heard the music but I didn't dance. I had started to see the pattern: anyone inside the progressive coalition is defined as all good and anyone outside it is all bad. By the time Trump arrived, I had learned not to give this message access to my eyes and ears. (This is explained in my book, *How I Escaped from Political Correctness, And You Can Too*.)

It's hard to believe you are following a template because the brain doesn't notice its own pathways. It's hard to question a template that everyone around you accepts. It's easier to see the pattern when you think of Marxism as a religion.

2

The Religion of Revolt

Religion fills many needs. It creates community. It offers hope. It defines good and evil in a way that makes you good. Karl Marx attacked religion, and then created a new religion to fill the vacuum.

Marx called religion, "the opiate of the masses." I was raised with religion, but I dropped it after my college professors ridiculed it in this way. The human mind needs structure, alas, so it's not surprising that so many people embrace the Marxist mindset once they spurn religion.

The worship service of the Marxist religion is protesting. Instead of going to church, temple or mosque, you are encouraged to join political action groups. You devote your time and money, you spread their doctrine, and whenever possible, you follow them into the streets. This makes you a good person in the eyes of other progressives.

Political action groups come in many varieties, just like religions. There are big organizations with big hierarchies, and small casual groups with friendly faces. Progressive action groups offer a banquet of opportunities to meet basic needs. They build solidarity, which meets the mammalian need for the safety of a herd. They create positive expectations about the future, which gratifies the mammalian urge to seek. And they give you a sense of moral superiority, which meets the mammalian need for social importance. The progressive religion can easily fill your life.

In the 1930s, the Soviet Union funded political action groups around the world. The Communist International recruited, trained and promoted on a massive scale. A wide array of groups was created so the movement could appeal to average people as well as committed revolutionaries. You had to rise in the socialist hierarchy before you had access to the revolutionary agenda. Many people strove to raise their status in this world because they saw it as prestigious. Important people were courted and wooed by socialist groups in order to "destroy the establishment from the inside." The movement gained important allies by treating them like superstars.

In the 1940s, the Nazi threat led to an alliance between the US and the Soviet Union. That made it possible to pass off Marxism as a contribution to the war effort. As war manufacturing grew, more factory workers were initiated into the progressive religion. After the war, consumer manufacturing grew, and the incitement of revolt among factory workers grew with it. Management often submitted to quell conflict.

By the 1960s, factory jobs were being overtaken by service jobs. Marxists would lose ground unless they expanded into new markets. Race and gender were seized on. The old victimhood template was repurposed for new identity groups instead of labor vs. management. The rewriting of the script was supported by abundant public funding for education and the arts. The "Amerika is evil" meme became entrenched in the culture.

Marxists would lose ground unless they expanded into new markets. Race and gender were seized on.

In 1991, the Soviet Union fell, depriving the movement of its presumed "better world." Without a clear promised land, progressive strategists built solidarity by focusing more on a common enemy: the straight white male. We suddenly heard endless messaging about the oppression suffered at the hands of SWMs. This was a calculated risk, since the movement could alienate SWMs by demonizing them. But the gamble worked. Plenty of SWMs submitted themselves to abuse in order to maintain social bonds and feel morally superior. This form of religious devotion continues.

The progressive religion has penetrated the culture so thoroughly that you may not know you are practicing it. Other religions openly name themselves, but the progressive religion hides behind a veil of science and ethics. Progressives claim to be "evidence-based," and mass produce "studies" that fit the agenda. They invoke ethics while inciting believers to take from others. Science and ethics are used to persuade you that you serve the greater good when you attack enemies. In the progressive religion, you are good no matter what you do if you are "disadvantaged," which is now defined to include 99% of us. Everything that happens to you is not your fault because progressive scriptures have evidence that it's society's fault.

You may still think people could not be following a dogma without knowing it. Here are some good reasons why it happens. There are so many reasons that it's hard to hope for us mammals to do otherwise.

1. Free stuff feels good.

The offer of free stuff lures a first step toward the progressive agenda. It could be cash, like government benefits and jobs, but there are many alternatives to cash. You can get grades that you haven't earned, or sexual opportunity, or public recognition, by joining the progressive alliance. The first time you accept free stuff, it feels so good that you want more. Once you invest your energy in the progressive agenda, you have less energy to build skills needed to get stuff on your own. You can easily become dependent on progressive leaders to meet your needs for you. They have a lot of free stuff to give because they get it from "the rich," both by controlling tax money and by extorting "the rich" with threats of violence.

2. Blame feels good.

The progressive mindset frees you from responsibility for your own life. Everything that happens to you is the fault of social injustice. You can give free rein to your animal impulses, and if there are bad consequences, you can blame "the system." You don't have to tackle your problems because you expect "social change" to fix everything.

3. Moral superiority feels good.

When you embrace the progressive religion, you can feel superior to everyone who is not progressive, no matter what you actually do with your life. Everything you do is morally superior as long as you say it fights injustice. Some people do more for the cause than you do, of course, so you may feel pressured to keep up. You look for ways to demonstrate your commitment to the fight in order to

When you embrace the progressive religion, you can feel superior no matter what you do.

sustain your one-up feelings. Happy chemicals are quickly metabolized, so you have to do it again and again to keep feeling it. You can end up investing a lot of your energy in this religion.

4. Social support feels good.

Mammals seek safety in numbers because it promotes survival. We have inherited a brain that feels threatened when isolated. There are fast ways and slow ways for mammals to build social bonds. Fast bonds form when a predator lurks. When the threat eases, mammals bond slowly from repeated acts of reciprocal trust. Humans have always bonded around common enemies because it's so effective. A sense of solidarity forms instantly without the hard work of one-to-one reciprocal trust. The progressive religion satisfies the urge for social support by focusing you on common enemies. But you pay a high price: perpetual fear.

5. Utopias feel good.

Our brain evolved to avoid threat, so it's natural to dream of a world that eliminates threatened feelings. You feel good as soon as you imagine the promised land of peace and love. You feel even better when you think you are moving toward it just by hanging with your friends to discuss your enemies. You feel like you've solved your problems when these good feelings flow, even if you have not done anything about your problems. Our ancestors would not have survived if they sat around imagining a perfect world instead of seeking food and shelter. But when the people around you are focused on utopias, it's hard to stay focused on the humdrum responsibilities of life.

6. Aggression feels good.

Animals are always looking for opportunities to be in the position of strength. They control their aggression because they don't want to get bitten or clawed by stronger individuals. Progressive messaging persuades you that you are a little monkey being victimized by bigger monkeys, and promises to reverse this if you follow progressive leaders. They offer you a safe way to vent frustrations at the people you are really mad at. You don't want to get bitten, so you need safe targets to attack. Progressive strategists are always there to help with a plan for the next target and the next attack.

7. Submitting to bullies feels good.

Bullies trigger fear, and submitting relieves the fear quickly. Animals submit to aggressors to avoid getting bitten or clawed. They make submission gestures to protect themselves from attack. We humans also submit to avoid conflict, and often do it with ritualized submission gestures. No one likes to admit they are submitting to a bully to protect themselves, so the verbal brain glorifies the bully or invents a greater good that submission serves.

Submissive animals often get protection from their stronger troop mates. Protection is the reward for submission. In childhood, protection allows us to survive, so our brains learn to promote survival by seeking protection later on. The progressive religion offers you protection as long as you submit to its dictates. This feels so natural that you may not notice yourself doing it.

8. Repetition is truth.

A repeated message feels true because "neurons that fire together, wire together." The messages repeated in your youth become the highways of your brain because neuroplasticity is higher then. Emotions are like paving on your neural pathways, so the emotional messages repeated in youth become the superhighways of your brain.

These pathways have more power than we imagine because the electricity in the brain flows into the pathways you have. Unfamiliar information is ignored because electricity has trouble flowing along unconnected neurons. We are not aware of our own neural pathways, however, so we think we are just responding to the facts of the world around us. We don't see how we're shaped by the repeated emotions of youth. And we don't notice the way we ignore truths that don't fit our old circuits.

Unfamiliar information is ignored because the brain's electricity has trouble flowing along uncon- nected neurons.

The brain evolved to motivate survival action, not to make you happy. It only releases happy chemicals in short spurts, so you always have to do more to get more. This helped our ancestors survive, but it leads to frustration if you are told that others get effortless happiness and you are deprived.

The good feeling of social dominance is released in short spurts. It's gone in a few minutes so you have to seek it again and again. Modern culture has taught us to expect good feelings all the time. When your happy chemicals dip, you're taught to think something is wrong. You think others are getting free happy chemicals and you are missing out. You expect the health care system or the political system to make you feel good instead of looking inside. This is the progressive religion. (More detail in my books: *I, Mammal: How to Make Peace With the Animal Urge for Social Power,* and in my forthcoming *Status Games: Why We Play and How to Stop.*)

You may say "So what? Progressive is just compassion. Socialism is just sharing. What could be wrong with that?"

3

What Harm Can in a Little Revolt Do?

We humans are born with rage– not the conscious rage you think in words, but the chemical rage released by your animal brain. Threat chemicals surge when you see a survival threat, but our brain defines survival in a quirky way. Consider the cries of a newborn baby. The baby is hungry but it can't do anything to meet its needs except to cry. Crying is a big surge of cortisol, often called the "stress chemical." We are designed to surge with cortisol when we fail to meet a need. Controlling that cortisol is the task of being human.

A child starts to control its cortisol in an interesting way. When a newborn cries, a liquid arrives in its mouth, and its hunger is relieved. The good feeling connects all the neurons active at that moment. The next time the baby hears its mother's footstep, a good feeling turns on because a pathway has been built. The baby doesn't yet know what milk is, or what people are, but it has wired in expectations about meeting its needs.

It takes a long time to wire a human brain with the skills necessary to meet its survival needs. Humans have longer childhoods than animals because we have more neurons and less hard wiring. A gazelle can run with the herd the day it's born. A newborn elephant walks to reach its mother's nipple. Humans are more helpless and vulnerable at birth than other creatures. Exploding with rage is the only skill we're born with. (This is elaborated in my book, *Tame Your Anxiety: Rewiring Your Brain for Happiness.*)

People have struggled to manage this impulse since our species began. Tantrums are natural in toddlers, but better ways to meet needs are gradually wired in. Each brain wires itself to seek rewards wherever it has gotten rewards before. This complicates life a lot. Tantrums continue if they are rewarded, and if alternatives are not rewarded. Repetition builds the pathway that activates tantrums without conscious intent.

Each brain faces the world with the pathways it has. After adolescence, neuroplasticity declines and new pathways are harder to build. A society that rewards tantrums can end up with a lot of people who have not wired in the skills necessary to meet their needs.

Animals learn survival skills at a young age because nobody feeds them, except for mother's milk. A little monkey doesn't get solid food unless it finds its own, yet every monkey manages to wire in foraging skills before lactation ends. Each success triggers happy chemicals, which motivates the next step. The mammal brain saves the happy chemicals for survival action, not to make you feel good about sitting on the couch.

The progressive religion suggests that you shouldn't have to do something unless you think it's "fun." If you do not study in school, you can blame the system for failing to make it fun. If you do not work, you can blame the system for failing to offer you a fun job. If you do not maintain social bonds, you can blame other people's "insensitivity" for making it un-fun.

The progressive religion suggests that you shouldn't have to do something unless you think it's "fun."

Unfortunately, fun is a poor guide to happy chemicals in the long run. Your brain doesn't reward you with happy chemicals unless you take action to meet your needs. If you expect the system to meet your needs for you, you deprive yourself of happy chemicals.

The progressive religion trains you to see your unmet needs as evidence that the system has failed. It prepares you for a life of disappointment. It rewards you with the comfort of other disappointed ("like-minded") people, and assurances of your moral superiority. But it deprives you of the natural pleasure of actin to meet your own needs.

Students learn to blame the system in school. Every kid can figure out how to get a grade by critiquing the system instead of doing the work. Each time you're rewarded for a boilerplate critique, you have less incentive to seek rewards by building useful skills. Skill deficits result, and you need to critique the system more and more to navigate around them. When your only tool is a hammer, you see everything as a nail. By the time you finish school, you may be good at victim olympics, but you may lack the math skills necessary to cut a recipe in half.

This is not sustainable. Progressive politics is like a Ponzi scheme or multi-level marketing. You can live the good life if you keep recruiting enough new people to invest all they have in your scheme. You recruit them by selling the dream of a system that meets your needs for you. This dream is easy to embrace because your needs were met for you in childhood. Progressives do not overtly promote child-like dependence in adult; they simply ridicule personal responsibility as a remnant of the failed capitalist system. This view of adulthood becomes the law of the land if 51% of voters are persuaded to embrace it. But this view of adulthood can never be sustainable.

Today, 51% of voters in most democracies are government dependents already. But you still have a choice. You can get real about your brain and your life, whether the herd does or not.

The progressive mindset is unsustainable from a mental-health perspective as well as an economic perspective. The system cannot make you happy. The act of meeting your needs is what stimulates happy chemicals. Progressive policies lead to dependence and unhappiness. Progressivism doesn't make sense unless your goal is to create an army of discontent to increase your own power. It serves progressive leaders, not the greater good.

The system cannot make you happy. The act of meeting your needs is what stimulates happy chemicals. Progressive policies lead to dependence and unhappiness.

The world was not perfect before Marxism. We humans have always been mammals. Marxism was just a new way to build a herd to dominate a common enemy. Monkeys prevail when their social alliance is bigger than their rivals' alliance, so natural selection built a brain that rewards you with a good feeling when you build alliances.

We naturally long for the comfort of moral superiority and a strong social alliance. But when you meet these needs through submission to the progressive religion, you pay a high price.

As I pondered my choices, I learned more about my own history. My grandfather was born in the cradle of the Mafia in Sicily. The Mafia was hardly mentioned when I was growing up. Italians said it didn't exist– that Hollywood and the police just invented it. But I finally learned that the Mafia is quite real. It stole from its own people for centuries, and killed those who didn't submit. Despite these atrocities, Mafiosi managed to glorify themselves in the eyes of Sicilians by presenting themselves as protection from "the real enemy"– the rich and powerful outside Sicily.

I learned that my grandfather's town lacked running water and flush toilets until the 1950s. Most people were illiterate, and their children had malnutrition and worms. Most important, they had an endless cycle of violence. When the US poured aid into Italy after World War II, the Mafia stole it. Heroin trafficking finally brought prosperity to my grandfather's town in the 1980s. Fortunately for me, my grandfather left in 1910. He went to the coal mines of Ohio, then sold fruit in Brooklyn, and finally opened a shop selling new high-tech products–televisions and refrigerators.

When Italians earned money, the Mafia tried to take a cut of it. Those who resisted were brutally attacked. Law enforcement slowly eroded Mafia power thanks to a few brave individuals. If it weren't for them, my life would have been shaped by the Mafia. Unfortunately, mafias are widespread around the world today. They prey on their own people by presenting themselves as protection from "the real enemy." You tolerate their predation and even glorify them to avoid harm. You blame outsiders for the sorry state of affairs.

The temptation to join a mafia makes sense from a mammalian perspective. It's tempting to seek immediate glory instead of taking the bus to work like an Average Joe. Fortunately, many people have learned to resist that impulse. Many people have taught their children to meet their needs in better ways.

But the concept of "revolution" has been glamorized by progressive educators and media. Textbooks and movies create a glorious impression of the revolutions in France, Russia, China, and Cuba. They skim over the massive death toll of these revolutions. Some of those deaths came from the initial fight for power; some from brutal in-fighting among "revolutionaries"; some from mobs rioting with impunity for decades; and some from famine caused by the chaos.

These facts are secret in Communist countries, and speaking of them lands you in prison. The freedom of information we enjoy today is a precious hard-won gift from our ancestors. Yet we're tempted to ignore information that doesn't fit the progressive template because social ostracism is scary and utopian visions are alluring.

Progressives construct statistics to back their assertions, and few people challenge statistics. Most of our statistics come from university and media elites who fear excommunication if they deviate from the progressive agenda. Few people are willing to risk career suicide, so if you rely on widely reported statistics, you only get information that fits the progressive agenda.

But you have power over the information you let into your brain. You can decide whether to seek good feelings by following the progressive herd or by meeting your own needs. If you let the progressive template shape your reality, you will end up bitter and resentful.

It's tempting to rage when the world disappoints your expectations. It's tempting to mirror the emotions of others because we're born with mirror neurons designed to do that. But each brain has billions of extra neurons waiting to connect into new pathways. You can find your power to feel good by creating for yourself instead of by destroying what others have created. (This is the subject of my book, Habits of a *Happy Brain: Retrain your brain to boost your serotonin, dopamine, oxytocin and endorphin levels* and *The Science of Positivity: Stop Negative Thought Patterns By Changing Your Brain Chemistry.*)

You can feel good by creating for yourself instead of by destroying what others have created.

4

Overlooked Information

We decide what is true with our old neural pathways, which makes it easy to reject new information. To have fresh insight, it helps to read the life stories of others. But the stories you hear in the media and education are all about oppression and injustice, so it's hard to see life in other ways. Here is a list of alternatives– books that helped me understand the animal urge to revolt all around us.

Radical Son: A Generational Odyssey
by David Horowitz

This book had a huge impact on my thinking. Horowitz was a "red diaper baby," which means his parents were in the American Communist Party. They were always going to Party meetings, so he grew up playing with the children of other Communists outside meeting rooms. These children became the leaders of the 1960s revolts.

Horowitz was a prominent sixties "radical" until the Black Panthers killed a friend of his. He had actively supported the Panthers, so when they needed an accountant, he recommended a friend. He was horrified to learn that they killed her in order to cover up information. He tried to tell people, but no one would listen. Suddenly, he saw the hypocrisy in the movement and distanced himself. He lost most of his relationships as a result. I faced a similar dilemma when I stopped following "the Party line," so the book was very helpful for me.

Rivethead: Tales from the Assembly Line
by Ben Hamper

This book played a big role in my understanding of human nature. Hamper was a factory worker who was able to quit his day job when his essays on life as an autoworker became popular. Instead of being happy, he had a breakdown. This helped me see how people blame their unhappiness on popular targets because they don't understand their own deeper workings. People resist rules when they have them, but without rules they fall apart.

The author explains his early life in detail, so it's easy to see the foundations of his distress. The book shows how he kept himself together despite severe addictions when he needed the job to support his family. As soon as he was his own boss, he collapsed. We're supposed to blame General Motors for his breakdown, but it's clear that he needed the structure of his job to function. The book describes the shockingly dysfunctional work habits in the auto plant and the union's role in enabling these destructive practices.

Last of the Cold War Spies: The Life of Michael Straight— the Only American in Britain's Cambridge Spy Ring

by Roland Perry

This book was deeply meaningful to me because the spy's name was on the building I walked through every day as a Cornell undergraduate. The building was funded by the same family money that sent this young man to Cambridge, where he helped the Soviet Union undermine Western governments. Then he was Editor of The New Republic Magazine, and Deputy Chair of the US National Endowment for the Arts. This book showed me that espionage allegations are not just the fantasy of "right-wing nuts." And it confirmed what I'd learned about the link between culture and Marxism.

The building named after Michael Straight's father played an oddly pivotal role in my life. That building was taken over by armed members of Cornell's Afro-American Society in 1969. A photo of them holding rifles in front of the building won a Pulitzer Prize and was printed everywhere. A few months later, I was called in to my guidance counselor's office to talk about which colleges to apply to. The counselor recommended Cornell. I can't help but thinking that many families steered away from Cornell that year, and my counselor was on the receiving end of a marketing pitch. But it worked out great for me so I'm eternally grateful to that counselor.

History Lesson: A Race Odyssey
by Mary Lefkowitz

This is the story of a college professor who was attacked for disagreeing with the progressive agenda. Her colleague at Wesley was teaching that Ancient Greeks stole their ideas from Egypt, and that slavery was organized by Jews. Lefkowitz was a Classics professor, and saw these assertions as factual errors. When she expressed disagreement, she was shunned by colleagues and administrators. She continued to express herself, and was attacked on many fronts. I was a college professor for 25 years, so her description of academia's preference for ideology over truth is very real to me.

Witness

by Whittaker Chambers

This is the classic story of a man who joined the American Communist Party and worked his way up to high-level espionage for the Soviet military. He quit, at great risk to his life, when he understood the scale of Stalin's purges. He became a household word when he was called to testify on the alleged espionage of top FDR advisor, Alger Hiss. In this book, Chambers describes his association with Hiss and with Communism in great detail. There's no tone of boasting or preaching, and I found it convincing.

Two points really shook me. One was Chamber's first job in the movement, as 1925 editor of the Communist newspaper, the Daily Worker. They sat Chambers next to the Associated Press wire (it was literally a wire then!) and told him to look for the class-warfare angle in each story. Today, when I hear the news, it's clear to me that I am only hearing the class-warfare angle.

I was also jolted by Chambers's assertion that the State Department and White House were full of Communists and sympathizers. This is how Alger Hiss could be at the top of the State Department, and thus FDR's advisor in talks with Stalin at Yalta. Other sources confirm that Hiss actually met privately with Stalin to receive instructions. This was chilling for me because my graduate school was established as training for the State Department, and I seriously considered working there. It was all the more personal because Chambers grew up where I grew up, so his stomping grounds were quite familiar.

Hollywood Traitors: Blacklisted Screenwriters
by Alan Ryskind

I grew up with the left-wing perspective on the McCarthy hearings— that right-wing nuts inflicted a travesty of justice on innocent people. But when I watch old movies, I can see that they're full of Marxist memes. I was glad to find a book that explained the Communist Party's control over screenwriters in the early days of Hollywood. The author is the son of one of those screenwriters. He details the role of Soviet agents in the daily lives of writers and of Hollywood. The Party's control over the its members shocked me, as did the willingness of believers to submit to that control.

The Gulag Archipelago
by Aleksandr Solzhenitsyn

"Gulag" is the Russia word for prison camp. The author is a Nobel-prize winning survivor of these camps. So many camps were spread throughout the Soviet Union that he calls them an archipelago. Before this 1973 book, you were still considered a right-wing nut if you acknowledged the brutality of life in the Soviet Union. Those who like to idealize socialist countries are quick to call the US a police state, so everyone should read this book before using such terms. I am grateful to Prof. Richard Lourie for forcing me to read it, though it was a nightmarish experience at the time.

Ex-Friends
by Norman Podhoretz

Podhoretz was an insider in New York intellectual circles. This group of famous writers was so close that they were known as "the Family." When Podhoretz had an opinion that didn't conform to their unanimous left-wing views, he was vilified and excommunicated. This book describes his falling out with each of these well-known writers. It's trashy celebrity gossip, perhaps, but it's different from the progressive celebrity gossip we're accustomed to.

The opinion that got Podhoretz banished was his observation that America is full of opportunity. He had built himself a great career despite his impoverished origins. He wanted to celebrate the system that makes this possible instead of condemning it. That was a sin to those who practiced the religion of victimhood. The argument itself is explained in his earlier book, *Breaking Ranks: A Political Memoir*.

Mao: The Unknown Story
by Jung Chang

Mao was heroized in my world. I figured there was more to the story but I never really knew it. Then I noticed this book from the celebrated author of *Wild Swans*. It was devastatingly sad. I could only get through it because I listened to it while driving or walking, and because I had studied China for most of my life so I longed to complete the puzzle.

The bottom line is that Mao was never a hero to anyone who knew him. He seized power by cozying up to Stalin while the leaders of the Chinese Communist Party sought independence from Moscow. Stalin channeled funding to Mao, so the Party needed him to survive. Mao knew how to kowtow to the alpha gorilla, but was also a master at attacking allies as soon as he didn't need them. Thus he ended up with a monopoly on power.

We often see images of Mao receiving adulation from massive crowds. This book provides the disheartening story behind the scenes. Mao had learned the cult of personality from Stalin. People risked imprisonment if they refused to participate in Mao worship. The book helps you understand how people can be manipulated on a massive scale. The tortures used by Chinese governments before and during Mao's rule is a sad thread running through it.

God and Man at Yale
by William F. Buckley

This 1951 book is an antidote to the belief that politicized universities are a new thing. Buckley wrote it to inform his fellow Yale alumni of the anti-free-market and anti-religious views of Yale faculty. I do not share his view that Yale should teach "Christian" values, but it is a fact that Yale began as a training school for Christian ministers, and embraced Christianity for 250 years. Imagine if you went to a school with a 250-year tradition and then it hired professors who ridiculed your values. You may agree with the politics of your professors, so let's consider an apolitical example. Let's say your school hires professors who think suicide is a reasonable response to life's frustrations. Would you want to know this as you donate money to your alma mater? Would you want to know this before sending your kids there?

The point of this book is not to tell the university what to teach, but to tell trustees and alumni what is actually going on. Buckley explains that professors do not openly espouse Marxism because "Marx himself, in the course of his lifetime, envisaged two broad lines of action that could be adopted to destroy the bourgeoisie: one was violent revolution; the other a slow increase of state power…."

Some background on the 1951 perspective is needed. US policy in World War II is critiqued so much today that we forget the huge visceral threats that it relieved. The United States had good reason to develop an atomic bomb because Germany was seeking one, and because Japan vowed to fight to the last man. A few months after the US bomb was built, Russians exploded a similar device. Americans upgraded that bomb a few years later, and again the Russians quickly followed. It was not hard to see how Communists got the technology since they had ties with high-profile atomic scientists in the US. Today, you may think of Communists as harmless idealists, but in 1951, they had just seized half of Europe and killed or jailed millions in the process.

Heart of the Dog
by Mikhail Bulgakov

This brilliant Russian satire explores the animal origins of our political impulses, which makes it eerily close to home. It's about a dog with transplanted human glands. The dog turns into a classic corrupt official, who speaks in politically correct lingo while taking from others to feather his own nest. It was written inside the Soviet Union in 1925, but not published for sixty years. Socialists have always claimed that they would create a "new man" without the greed inherent in capitalism. Their theory is undermined by the greed of government bureaucrats in socialist environments.

The God That Failed:
Why Six Great Writers Rejected Communism
ed. by Richard H. Crossman

In this 1952 book, six high-profile writers explain why they joined the Communist Party, and why they left it. These writers shared the same urge that we have to make a better world, and the same fear we have of being socially shunned.

Their autobiographical sketches remind us of the Party's absolute power over its members. If you joined, you had to submit completely to the party bureaucrat assigned to monitor you. Most important, you owed loyalty to the Soviet Union rather than to your country of citizenship. Bad things happened to people who didn't follow "the Party line" on every issue. No matter where you lived, you joined a totalitarian state when you became a member. That would feel very one-down, but you restored your one-up feeling with moral superiority and strength in numbers.

The War on Cops: How the New Attack on Law and Order Makes Everyone Less Safe
by Heather MacDonald

Unlike the rest of this list, this book relies statistics rather than biography. It shows that residents of high-crime neighborhoods welcome police protection, and suffer terribly when protective policing is withdrawn. MacDonald challenges charges of police racism with overlooked studies on crime from progressive sources. The full story is quite different from the story that has been reported. We need these facts before letting our mammal brains to jump to conclusions.

My books about the Mammal Brain

Habits of a Happy Brain:
Retrain Your Brain to Boost Your Serotonin,
Dopamine, Oxytocin and Endorphin Levels

Tame Your Anxiety:
Rewiring Your Brain for Happiness

How I Escaped from Political Correctness, and
You Can Too

I, Mammal:
How to Make Peace With the Animal Urge for
Social Power

The Science of Positivity:
Stop Negative Thought Patterns by Changing
Your Brain Chemistry

Status Games: Why We Play and How to Stop
(forthcoming)

About the Author

Loretta Graziano Breuning, PhD, is founder of the Inner Mammal Institute and Professor Emerita of Management at California State University, East Bay. She is the author of many personal development books, including Habits of a Happy Brain: Retrain Your Brain to Boost Your Serotonin, Dopamine, Oxytocin and Endorphin Levels.

As a teacher and a parent, she was not convinced by prevailing theories of human motivation. Then she learned about the brain chemistry we share with earlier mammals and everything made sense. She began creating resources that have helped thousands of people make peace with their inner mammal. Her work has been translated into Spanish, Russian, Chinese, Arabic, French, Turkish, and German, and cited in major media.

Dr. Breuning is a graduate of Cornell University and Tufts, and a grandparent of two. Before teaching, she worked for the United Nations in Africa.

The Inner Mammal Institute offers videos, books, podcasts, blogs, multimedia, and a training program, to help you make peace with your inner mammal. You can follow Dr. Breuning's work on YouTube, Facebook, PsychologyToday.com, LinkedIn,

Instagram and Twitter. Get a free five-day happy chemical jumpstart at: InnerMammalInstitute.org.

Manufactured by Amazon.ca
Bolton, ON